CHICHEN
ITZA

Cover:
The Castillo from
the Temple of the Jaguars

Photography:
Enrique Franco Torrijos
I.N.A.H.

First edition in english: 1981
Seventeenth reprint in english: 1991
© Panorama Editorial, S.A.
   Leibnitz 31, Col. Anzures
   11590 México, D.F.

Text:
   Lilian Scheffler

Translated by:
   David Castledine

PANORAMA GUIDEBOOKS
   Under the direction of:
   Federico Santiago E.

Photographs:
   Manuel Lozano
   Irmgard Groth
   Walter Reuter
   I.N.A.H.

Printed in Mexico
Impreso en México
ISBN 968-38-0003-3

CHICHEN
ITZA

PANORAMA EDITORIAL, S.A.

Index

How you can use this Guidebook

The archaeological zone of Chichen Itzá is located at the side of the Mérida-Valladolid-Cancún highway. The buildings of the Classic period of the Maya and of the Transitional period are situated to the south of the zone. Some of them pertain to the zone of Old Chichen, so called because it was the area that the inhabitants of the site first occupied, next to the Xtoloc *cenote,* or natural well, which provided drinking water.

In an area of approximately three kilometers long by two kilometers wide, there are many constructions. Only a small part of them has been explored, and the rest are covered by underbrush. In this area are found the constructions dating from the Classic Maya period, and more recent ones from the Maya-Toltec period.

The most important constructions of the Maya-Toltec period are almost all located in the northern part of the zone, near the two visitors' entrances and the new car park.

This guidebook is organized chronologically according to the historical-artistic periods: the Formative or Preclassic, the Classic, the Interregnum or Transitional, the Maya-Toltec and the period of Mexica absorption, without taking into account the importance of each monument in isolation, but rather the antiquity of the period concerned.

In the Table of Contents will be found the page numbers corresponding to the descriptions of each monument, so that the reader may choose between visiting the zone by following a strict chronological sequence or beginning with the buildings he considers most important.

At the end of this guidebook, the reader will find a very useful glossary of architectural terms and Maya words.

Light and Sound Show

This show, with commentaries in both Spanish and English, takes place most nights. It depicts the history of Chichen Itzá in a marvellous display of different coloured lights. For information on times it is best to enquire at the Dirección de Fomento Turístico (tourist office) in Mérida, Calle 59, N.º 490, (telephone 1-59-89). Alternatively, enquire at the zone itself.

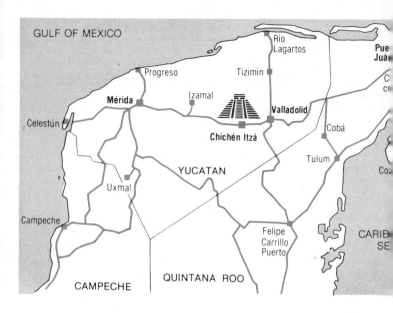

Geographical location

Chichen Itzá, one of the most important archaeological cities of the Maya culture, is situated 120 kilometers from Mérida, capital city of the State of Yucatan. The trip by automobile or passenger bus from the state capital to the archaeological ruins takes under two hours on the excellent Mérida-Valladolid-Cancún highway. Along this route are several towns in which one can see interesting churches —most of them partially destroyed during the War of the Castes, an uprising of the Maya in the middle of the nineteenth century— as well as old haciendas, henequen fields and several nearby *cenotes*. In these places one can buy different types of handicrafts and native costumes. Since this highway crosses fairly flat country and has few bends, the archaeological zone is easily reached and it is possible for visitors to return to Mérida the same day, if they wish.

Hotel accommodation

For those who wish to remain longer at Chichén Itzá, the following excellent hotels are located within the zone: *Hotel Hacienda Chichén, Hotel Mayaland,* and the *Archaeological Village* of the Club Mediterranée.

At a distance of three kilometers from the zone is the *Hotel Dolores Alba*, and in the town of Pisté, located two kilometers from the archaeological zone, are the *Hotel Cunanchen, Pirámide Inn, Posada Novelo,* and *Hotel Misión*, and also restaurants and handicraft shops.

General Information

The various projects that have been carried out in the archaeological zone have changed its appearance somewhat whilst at the same time ensuring the visitor's safety and comfort.

The Mérida-Valladolid highway no longer passes through the middle of the zone. It was recently rerouted and now skirts Chichen Itzá on the north side. Only the east and west accesses remain, barred by railings to stop vehicles entering the zone.

The car park and main entrance to Chichen Itzá are located near the Ball Court, together with toilets, restaurants, crafts shops and the ticket office.

By the Holy Well and on the way to the Observatory there are two huts which have toilet facilities and where you can buy a drink, something to eat or crafts. These palm-leaf thatched huts, resembling the old Mayan dwellings, provide particularly valuable facilities for the visitor to Chichen Itzá.

At travel agencies in the city of Mérida or in the archaeological zone itself, one may engage the services of guides for taking visitors to the zone and explaining the monuments and their history.

Since Chichen Itzá is situated in a sub-tropical region, it sometimes rains very heavily in the summer and autumn. However, hot, sunny days predominate throughout the year.

Outdoor photographs only are permitted, without the use of a tripod and for non-commercial purposes. For more elaborate photographic or movie equipment including tripods, dollies, cranes, artificial lighting, movie cameras, as well as 8mm. and super 8mm. filming gear, etc., it is necessary to request and obtain permission from the National Institute of Anthropology and History whose address is Córdoba N.º 45, México 7, D.F. At this same institute, special permission may also be requested for remaining in the archaeological zone at night or for entering before the official visiting hours.

The archaeological zone is open from 8am to 5pm. The interior of certain monuments may be visited at the following times:

The mural paintings in the Temple of the Jaguars may be visited from 10 to 11am and from 3 to 4pm. The interior of the Castillo may be visited from 11am to 1pm and from 4 to 5pm. Visits to the inside of the Temple of the Warriors have been temporarily suspended.

Visiting hours for the interesting Balankanchen Caves, located 4½ kilometers from Chichen Itzá, on the highway to Cancún, are the following: 8 till 11am and 2 to 4pm. except Sunday, when morning visits only are allowed.

THE MAYAS

The Maya

The extensive territory occupied by the Maya culture in Middle America covered approximately 325,000 square kilometers, and included the Mexican states of Yucatan, Campeche, Quintana Roo, Tabasco and the eastern part of Chiapas, as well as the major part of Guatemala (except for the Pacific coastal strip), Belize (British Honduras) and the western regions of Honduras and El Salvador.

The Maya race was made up of various groups who had more or less the same ethnic characteristics, and very similar physical features—all of whom had inherited the same culture. There were, however, differences from one region to another. One of the most notable of these was the diversity of languages, even though these were branches of a common linguistic stock. At present some 24 Maya languages are spoken in the region.

The Maya settled their territory in the same way that almost all pre-Columbian peoples did. They constructed ceremonial centers, surrounding which the priests and nobles lived permanently in palaces that were built in ceremonial areas. Thanks to recent archaeological explorations and studies, we know how the upper classes lived in Mayan cities, although we know very little about how the subjugated or lower classes, such as the peasants, lived and supported the powerful members of their society. In general terms, the chronology of Maya culture follows the chronology of Middle American culture, but its different periods can be divided more precisely, owing in part to the fact that the Maya dated their stelae by means of a chronological system, with paintings and ceramics. A careful reading of these yields nearly exact dates of numerous historical facts and makes it possible to determine the age of materials and objects of various types. According to J. Eric S.

Head of a person; Palenque, Chiapas.

Mayan gods; the god of human sacrifices,
The god of rain, and the god of death.

9

Thompson (*The Rise and Fall of Maya Civilization*, Mexico City, Fondo de Cultura Económica, 1959), one of the top authorities on Maya culture, the following periods comprise the chronological classification of Maya civilization.*

1) Formative or Preclassic Period

This period lasted from around 500 B.C. to 325 A.D. In other parts of Middle America it is called Late Preclassic or Protoclassic Period. During this period the Maya were unable to free themselves from the influence of neighboring peoples, mainly the Olmec. The first ethnic Maya features are perfectly delineated on clay figurines. During this period places flourished in the Maya area like Uaxactún, Tikal, Holmul, San José, the Altar of Sacrifices, in Central America; and Puuc, Yaxuná, Maní, Acanceh, Dzibilchaltún and Loltún, in the Yucatan Peninsula.

No construction at Chichén Itzá has been found from this period, and only the pottery called Chicanel has been identified.

2) Classic Period

This period lasted from 325 to 925 A.D., and is subdivided into three phases: Early Phase (325-625 A.D.); Flowering or High Classic Phase (625-800 A.D.) and Decline or Late Classic Phase (800-925 A.D.)

During the Early Phase, the typical characteristics of Maya culture appear: the construction of temples with the corbeled arch, and the measurement and cult of time, represented by the exact recording of its passage on stelae inscribed with both hieroglyphs and writing. Foreign influences disappear during this phase. Apart from those already mentioned above in the section on the Formative Period, sites that flourished are Usumacinta, in Central America, and in Yucatan, Santa Rosa, Cobá and Xtampac.

In Chichén Itzá no building dating from this phase has been identified. Only pottery contemporaneous with that of Tzakol has been found.

In the Flowering or High Classic Phase, everything is notably developed: architecture, sculpture, painting, ceramics, minor arts (lapidary, etc.), astronomy, mathematics, glyph-writing. Identified as belonging to this phase are the cities of Petén, Motagua, Palenque and Toniná. The sites of Chenes and Tancáh appear in Yucatan.

---

* On the other hand, Sylvanus G. Morley (*Maya Civilization,* Mexico City, F.C.E., 1947) affirms that Maya history can be divided into three general periods: 1) Preclassic, extending from approximately 1500 B.C. to 317 A.D.; 2) Classic, extending from 317 to 889 A.C.: and 3) Postclassic, from 889 to 1697 A.D.

Lintel 53 at Yaxchilán, Chiapas;
National Museum of Anthropology.

During the Flowering Phase one can speak of the first important occupation of Chichén Itzá, since the following were built there: the Nunnery complex with its annex, the Church, the Akab-Dzib, the Red House or Chichanchob, the House of the Deer, the Temple of the Phalluses, and the Temple of the Three Lintels. Also the pottery that is contemporaneous with that of Tepeu appears.

During the phase of decline, or Late Classic, the ceremonial centers are abandoned, perhaps on account of the influence of foreign peoples who slowly erode the Maya culture in such a way that the glory and splendor of the Flowering Phase is reduced to a level almost comparable to that of the Preclassic Period. Nonetheless, Putún characteristics appear in Seibal.

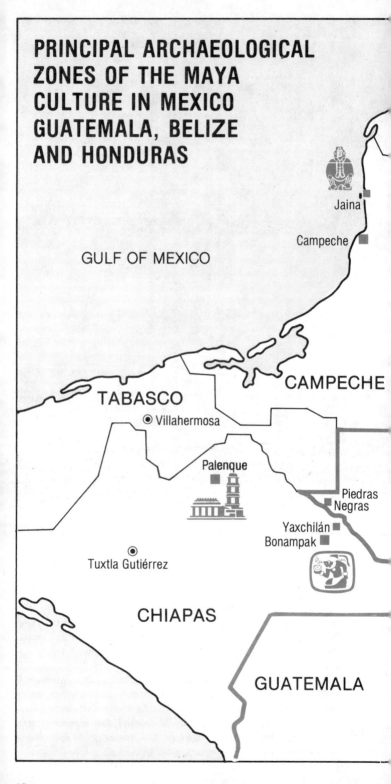

PRINCIPAL ARCHAEOLOGICAL ZONES OF THE MAYA CULTURE IN MEXICO GUATEMALA, BELIZE AND HONDURAS

Jaina

Campeche

GULF OF MEXICO

CAMPECHE

TABASCO

⊙ Villahermosa

Palenque

Piedras Negras

Yaxchilán
Bonampak

⊙ Tuxtla Gutiérrez

CHIAPAS

GUATEMALA

12

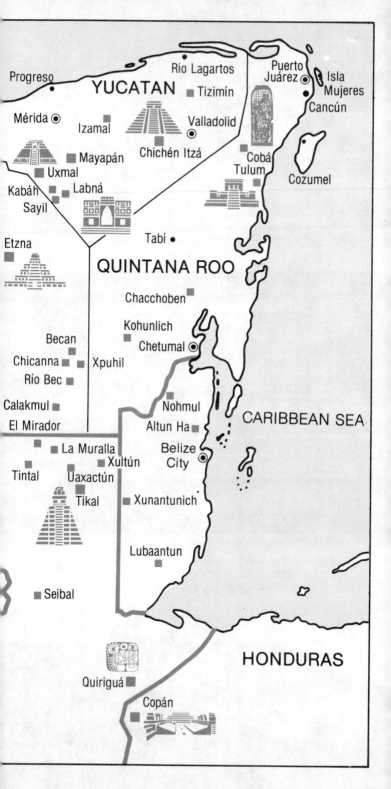

Progreso
YUCATAN
Río Lagartos
Tizimín
Puerto Juárez
Isla Mujeres
Cancún
Mérida
Izamal
Valladolid
Chichén Itzá
Cobá
Tulum
Cozumel
Mayapán
Uxmal
Kabáh
Sayil
Labná
Etzna
Tabí
QUINTANA ROO
Chacchoben
Kohunlich
Becan
Chetumal
Chicanna
Xpuhil
Río Bec
Calakmul
El Mirador
Nohmul
CARIBBEAN SEA
Altun Ha
La Muralla
Belize City
Xultún
Tintal
Uaxactún
Tikal
Xunantunich
Lubaantun
Seibal
HONDURAS
Quiriguá
Copán

13

3) Interregnum or Transitional Period

So called by Thompson, this period covers 50 years (925 to 975 A.D.). It is characterized by a sort of return to a very low cultural level, but the descendents of the Classic Maya undergo another historical process, in which their cultural heritage manifests itself, perhaps even more magnificently than before.

4) Mexica or Maya-Toltec Period

This period extends from 975 to 1200 A.D. and is distinguished by the introduction of cultural elements foreign to Maya civilization which originate in Tula and the Toltec culture.

In this period the cult of Quetzalcóatl (in the Náhua language, 'plumed serpent') is introduced, which, upon reaching the Yucatan Peninsula, is known by the Maya name of Kukulcán. The first Toltec features appear in the Mayan architecture of Uxmal and Kabah. Later, places like Izamal, Mayapán, Tihó, Champotón and Tayasal, all flourish. Chichén Itzá achieves architectural splendor; at the beginning comes the unique construction of the Caracol. Then follow the spectacular monuments with a marked blending of Maya and Toltec elements—of the Castillo, the Temple of the Warriors, the Ball Court, and buildings of less importance: the Tzompantli, the Temple of Venus, the Temple of Eagles and Jaguars, the Ossuary, the Temple of the Tables. In addition, the fine orange and lead-colored pottery makes its appearance.

5) Period of Mexica absorption

This period is also called Late Postclassic. It lasted from 1200 to 1540 A.D. It is characterized by alliances between Maya families and families of Náhua or Mexica origin, the last of which was formed between the cities of Uxmal, Mayapán and Chichén Itzá, which divided the Maya and ended in a bloody conflict—the attack and conquest of Chichén Itzá by the Cocomes of Mayapán and their revolt against the Xius of Uxmal.

When the Spanish arrived, they found a poor, divided land that was but a pale reflection of its former splendor. Chichén Itzá had lost its hegemony, and Mayapán ruled over the other Mayan centers. The Maya Toltec architectural style of Chichén Itzá was imitated elsewhere, and sites in the eastern part of the Yucatan Peninsula arose, such as Tulum and others of less importance.

Temple of the Sun; Palenque, Chiapas.

The Governor's Palace; Uxmal, Yucatán.

Tulum, Quintana Roo.

From this period there are no important constructions in Chichén Itzá, nor other cultural manifestations except the so-called Mayapán pottery, and some offerings found in the Sacred Cenote.

Architecture

Mayan architecture had its beginnings at a time when Mayan culture was still free from foreign influences—that is, in the Formative Period up to about 900 A.D. The pattern was set by a monument found in the city of Uaxactún, to the north of Tikal, the largest city of Mayan civilization. This monument has been given the name of E-VII sub, of Group E of that city. Following the custom of the Maya, this building was covered by another pyramid. Since the latter was destroyed, the archaeologists decided to remove it, thus exposing the older construction, or ''sub''.

The sub is a rectangular-shaped construction, surmounted by superimposed terraces, with elaborately-designed stairways flanked by balustrades adorned with large jaguar masks, which possibly represent the Rain God. It unquestionably reveals a style that is completely Olmec. One must speak of it as exclusively a tributary art. The entire mound formed by the sub was covered with polished stucco, and the upper part supported a temple that has disappeared, leaving only traces of its supports. In the upper part were found the holes where posts supporting the temple were fitted, and it was thanks to these that it was possible to rebuild the temple.

While it is true that in the Classic Period the characteristic element of Mayan architecture—the corbeled arch—appeared, it is also true that other elements (moldings, columns and cresting, together with superimposed terraces) were combined to create the different Mayan architectural styles. The principal such styles were the following:

1) The Petén Style

The buildings rise on superimposed, stepped terraces, with stairways projecting from the facade. Decorations of stuccoed masks are often used. Solid walls predominate over openings, producing thick walls and narrow rooms. There are very high crestings on the rear walls of temples, and facades with stucco decorations. This style is common in such cities as Uaxactún, Tikal, Piedras Negras, Nakum and Calakmul.

2) The Palenque Style

Characterized by vertical foundations; stairways framed by balustrades; temples containing two chambers, the rear chamber

Maya arch; Labná, Yucatán.

being the sanctuary; crestings resting on the central wall; facades with friezes parallel to the arches and decorated with stucco figures; predominance of openings over solid walls; This style is found in such cities as Palenque, Toniná, Copán, Quiriguá, Yaxchilán, Bonampak and Lacanjá.

3) The Rio Bec Style

This is a style that is primarily ornamental, seen in the stylisation of the pyramidal foundations with well-defined stairways that simulate ornamental towers. Stone mosaics are used as in Xpuhil, Río Bec, Hormiguero and Becán.

4) The Chenes Style

Features foundations of stepped bodies forming a slope; spaces divided by columns and vertical friezes; crestings on the front part of buildings; very complex ornamentation, with elements representing cabins, panels of frets, lattices, little drums and columns, large masks of the Rain God — all made of cut and assembled stone mosaic. This style is found in such cities as Hochob, Edzná and Xcalumkin.

5) The Puuc Style

This is similar to the Chenes style, with the difference that the ornamentation is not complete on the facades, but only on the friezes, and is based on stone mosaic that is very well cut, carved and fitted. This style abounds at Chichén Itzá.

6) The Mexica Style

This style results from the Toltec inflence in the northern Maya area, though it has some similarities to the Puuc style. Its features are foundations and platforms with high slopes and panels or cornices; stairways with serpents' heads at the foot of the balustrades; altars decorated with skulls; and serpent columns. It is found in such cities as Chichén Itzá, Tulum, Mayapán, Cobá, Acanceh and in other sites in Yucatan and Quintana Roo.

Sculpture and Ceramics

Being among the most notable manifestations of Maya art, their sculpture and ceramics were done in stucco, clay, jade, wood, and precious metals.

Carvings were made on stelae, panels, lintels, facades, door jambs, columns, stairways, and so on.

The masks and sculptures represent human figures, gods, priests, atlantes, etc. The carvings in high and low relief, and the ceramic pieces produced for religious purposes or for common use, are of extraordinarily fine artistic quality. A large part of the sculpture and pottery was given a polychrome finish.

Painting

Mainly decorative, Maya painting also had a religious, ritualistic or historical content. In architecture, wall frescoes were used a great deal. Painting was also done on codices, pottery, stuccos, columns and facades to represent both mythological and religious scenes and realistic, descriptive and narrative scenes depicting war, landscapes, animals and customs.

Writing

For a long time it was thought that Maya writing possessed characters that could be interpreted phonetically. The truth is that this hypothesis has not yet been definitely proven. The mathematical and chronological hieroglyphs have, however, been more

Female figure; Jaina, Campeche.

Detail of a mural painting; Bonampak, Chiapas
Copy in the National Museum of Anthropology.

successfully deciphered. For instance, it has been demonstrated that the Maya had three ideograms or basic arithmetical symbols; the dot ● has a numerical value of 1, the bar ▬ a numerical value of 5, and a stylized shell ⬭ symbolizes zero. The combination of these elements gave them the basis for a system based on twenty, from 0 to 19, assigning a relative value to the signs according to their position. This advanced system, and the use of zero, were used by the Maya centuries before any other culture in the world.

The chronological glyphs demonstrate the great determination of the Maya to record the passage of time. They developed astronomy to such a degree that they were able to use the most accurate calendar ever known to man. This was the solar calendar (called HAAB) consisting of 365 days and a fraction, divided into 18 months of 20 days each, plus one extra period of 5 days to round off the annual cycle—all worked out with mathematical precision.

Each day and month had a different name, related to some deity.

The Maya also had another calendar, of a ritualistic type (called TZOLK'IN), which had 260 days, with 20 cycles of 13 days each. The days had the same names as those of the solar calendar, but the names of the 13-day periods were different. In both calendars the Maya established an initial date for calculating years, which has been identified as 4 AHAU (ritual calendar), 8 CUMKU (solar calendar), and has been translated as corresponding to the year 3113 B.C.

Eclipse of the Maya Civilization

The Pre-Columbian Maya civilization in the Northern Yucatan Peninsula came to an end in 1540, when the city of Tihó fell into the hands of the Spanish conqueror Francisco de Montejo, who founded the city of Mérida on that site. In the south, the last Maya city to be founded, by the Itzás, located on the far west side of Lake Petén in Guatemala, was taken in 1697 by Martín Ursúa, the Governor of Yucatan, thus bringing to an end the independence of the Itzás, who were under the command of their chieftain, Canek.

Tombstone at the Temple of the Sun; Palenque, Chiapas.

Glyphs at the Forgotten Temple; Palenque, Chiapas.
Palenque Regional Museum.

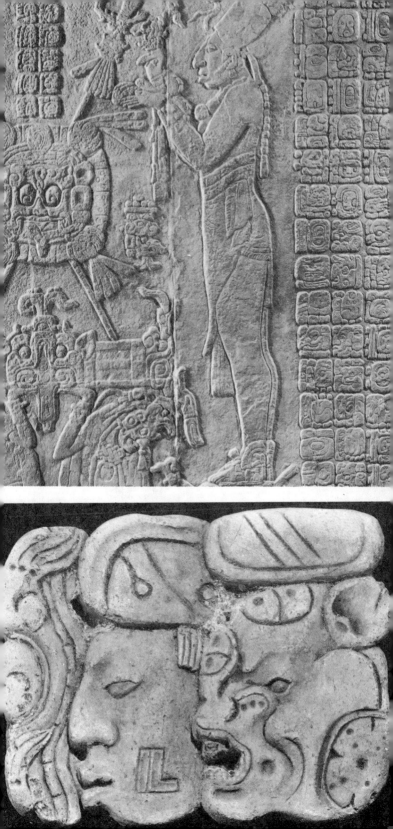

The Nunnery.

The Castillo or Pyramid of Kukulcán.
Lithographs by F. Catherwood.

CHICHEN ITZA

Explorations

Although references to the Maya cities were made during the colonial era, such as those by Friar Diego de Landa, Chichén Itzá lay hidden in the underbrush until the early part of the nineteenth century. At that time, John Lloyd Stephens, an American writer, diplomat and archaeologist, rescued the Maya cities from the historical obscurity in which they had remained until then, with the publication of his two books *Incidents of Travel in Central America, Chiapas and Yucatan* (1841) and *Incidents of Travel in Yucatan* (1843). The extraordinary drawings of the monuments of Chichén Itzá made by Frederick Catherwood, Stephens's companion, also contributed decisively to this end.

Subsequent to this discovery (for the modern world) of the culture of the Maya, a succession of travelers and archaeologists visited the ruins of Chichén Itzá and made new studies. Among the more noteworthy of these may be mentioned Augustus Le Plongeon, the Frenchman Désiré Charnay, and the English naturalist Alfred Percival Maudslay, who dedicated himself to studying the Maya monuments from 1881 to 1894. He published the results of his research in a monumental work entitled *Biologia Centrali Americana*, (1889-1902). Similarly, the Austrian Teobert Maler left valuable documents, in the form of photographs taken between 1891 and 1892, on the state of the ruins of Chichén at that time.

At the beginning of this century the United States consul in the city of Mérida, Edward Herbert Thompson, acquired the lands of the hacienda on which the ruins of Chichén Itzá are located.

He explored the zone and had the Sacred Cenote dredged, from which he extracted many objects of great value, including bones, pottery, beads, artifacts of jade and gold, and so on, most of which are now in the Peabody Museum at Harvard Univerity, and some in the museums of the Mexican Republic. Subsequently, the Government of Mexico took legal possession of the ruins, and from 1923 until 1933, explorations were undertaken in collaboration with the Carnegie Institution of Washington, D.C. The most important buildings were restored during that period. Since the latter date, the Mexican Government has gone on with the work. At the present time, the archaeological zone of Chichén Itzá is one of the most complete examples of the splendid Maya culture.

Etymology

One of the most widely accepted theories as to the meaning of Chichén Itzá is that the name is composed of the Maya words "chi", or mouth; "chen", or well and "Itzá", the name of the people who settled there. Thus the meaning of Chichén Itzá is "mouth of the well of the Itzá" or "at the mouth of the well of the water wizard".

Since there are no surface rivers in the northern part of the Yucatan peninsula, this name is specifically related to the *cenote* or well of Xtoloc and the so-called Sacred Well.

The cult of the aquatic world, representd by Chac, god of rain, was predominant in Maya culture, and gave rise to innumerable propitiatory rites. In the crystal-clear waters the priests and diviners consulted the oracle and learned of the wishes of the gods. For this reason, perhaps, the Itzás have been known as "water wizards", or "water sorcerers".

The Itzás

Researchers and specialists in Maya culture have several theories regarding the uncertain origin of the itzá. The following summarizes the two main theories:

According to one theory, the Itzás were people of pure Maya stock who came to the peninsula of Yucatan from lands lying farther to the south (the Petén region of Guatemala). First they reached Bacalar Lagoon in Quintana Roo, (415-435 A.D.) and then went inland to Chichén in the years 435-495 A.D.

According to the second theory, the Itzás were Chontal-speaking Maya who in the past had mingled with the Mexica and other Nahuatl-speaking peoples.

Their origin has been placed on the west coast of the Yucatan Peninsula, specifically in Chakamputún (present-day Champotón, Campeche) From there, sailing around the Peninsula, they reached Cozumel and traveled inland as far as Chichén Itzá. It is said that all these voyages were undertaken for reasons of trade.

Costume of Chichén Itzá warriors.

Personage carved on a pilaster of the Temple of the Warriors.

Defeat of the Itzás by
Toltec warriors.
Scene in hammered relief
on golden disk found
in the Sacred Cenote.

Historical Chronology

Dr. Sylvanus Griswold Morley, one of the most outstanding investigators of Maya culture, summarizes his theory of the evolution of Chichén Itzá as follows:

415 to 435 A.D. Arrival of the Itzás at Bakhalal (Bacalar, Quintana Roo) in the southern part of the Yucatan peninsula.

455 to 495 A.D. Discovery of Chichén Itzá by the Itzás.

495 to 514 A.D. Occupation of Chichén Itzá by the Itzás.

514 to 692 A.D. Abandonment of Chichén Itzá by the Itzás.

692 to 731 A.D. The Itzás emigrate to the southern part of the Yucatan peninsula, settling in Champotón.

731 to 998 A.D. Occupation of Champotón by the Itzás.

968 to 987 A.D. Return of the Itzás to Chichén Itzá.

1194 to 1204 A.D. The Cocomes, led by Hunac Ceel, attack and conquer Chichén Itzá, thus breaking up the alliance (the Mayapán League) between the Itzás of Chichén, the Xius of Uxmal, and the Cocomes of Mayapán. Defeat and expulsion of the Itzás.

Social and economic organization

According to some historians, the Itzás''... came upon the scene like conquerors,'' overpowering the original inhabitants of the area surrounding the *cenote*, dividing up the land among their chieftains, and then wielded power and control for many years.

Society was ruled over by the supposed descendent of the god, who was simultaneously supreme judge, commander of the army and possibly high priest as well. His position was hereditary. In order to carry out his duties he was assisted by the minor chieftains of the town or city, and by a number of individuals of religious, political, judicial or military rank who comprised the upper class, who engaged in trade, and who alone possessed knowledge of astronomy, law, medicine, astrology, mathematics and so forth. This elite social class constituted the apparatus of the state, which, together with the important merchants and traders, exercised power by physical and ideological means, through militarism and religion.

The middle-class inhabitants of Chichén Itzá held minor administrative posts, engaged in small trading activities, were artisans or artists of various kinds, or were farmers growing cacao on a small scale.

The lower class was made up of serfs, who cultivated the lands of the lords and of the state, and porters or bearers, soldiers in wartime, peons or construction workers, and slaves.

The importance of Chichén Itzá lay in its trading activity, which was the basis of its economy. It controlled the raw materials, domestic products and local handicraft production of the region. Trade and units of value were subject to regulation, with cacao beans most highly prized, although colored shells, pieces of cotton cloth of a certain size, copper rattles, jade beads and quetzal feathers, among other items, were also used. Trading was carried out on market days and during religious festivities, with traders and merchants gathered in Chichén from all the Maya regions, and perhaps from as far distant as Panama and Colombia.

Mural painting on the Temple of the Warriors
that represents trade in Chichén Itzá. There is a copy
in the National Museum of Anthropology.

The religion

Kukulcán was the most important deity of the Itzás. A great many representations of this god are to be found at Chichén Itzá, where the later Toltec influence merged Kukulcán and his cult with Quetzalcoátl. Kukulcán took the form of the bird-serpent or plumed serpent, as he is represented in the cultures of the central highlands of Mexico.

Also very important was the worship of Chac*, god of rain, upon whom depended the success of harvests, and Itzamná, lord of the heavens, Ah Puch, god of death, and other gods both heavenly and of the underworld.

* Alberto Ruz L. asserts that Chac, god of rain, was "the most popular and most venerated of the gods, principally in the arid north of the Yucatan peninsula, where his mask with its snout-like curved nose is reproduced profusely. Chac not only symbolized rain, but also wind, thunder and lightning. In addition, he was divided into four deities corresponding to the four cardinal points each associated with a particular color (red for east, white for north, black for west and yellow for south). He was thoroughly beneficent, since it was up to him to guarantee the success of harvests". (*La civilización de los antiguos mayas* (*The Civilization of the Ancient Maya*), México, INAH, 1963).

Kukulcán; detail on a pilaster of the South Temple.

Stylized representation of Kukulcán; North Temple.

Representation of Kukulcán-Quetzalcóatl; panel of the Temple of the Warriors.

Urban Layout

The long intermittent periods of time over which construction took place at Chichén Itzá probably accounts for the urban dispersion, which in turn required a system of internal causeways to connect the ceremonial centers with each other, and with the resident population.

These causeways or *sacbés* (literally, "white roads") include the following: the road from "El Castillo" to the Sacred Well; from El Castillo to the Nunnery complex; from the Nunnery to the Temple of the Three Lintels; from the Caracol observatory to the Well of Xtoloc; from the Thousand Columns leading east; from behind the Chichén hacienda to the Temple of the Hieroglyphic Jambs, and finally, the one starting from the Ball Court leading west.

These were the main avenues of internal communication, but there must also have been many small secondary roads, apart from the fact that the principal group of buildings of the Maya-Toltec period was enclosed by a low wall.

Well of Xtoloc

The northern part of the Yucatan Peninsula is extremely dry, due to sparse rainfall and extensive underground drainage. Most of its water is obtained from the cenotes (*dzonot* in Maya), which are openings in the surface formed naturally by the sinking of the surface limestone strata and consequent exposure of underlying water channels. The existence of these wells are the principal explanation for the location of various important cities.

The Well or Cenote of Xtoloc, in Old Chichén, supplied the city with water. There were also a number of *chultunes* (cisterns) strategically located so as to supply the local population with drinking water.

At the edge of the cenote is a small temple with columns and a sanctuary.

Sacred Well or the Well of Sacrifices

Used exclusively for religious purposes, dedicated to Chac, the Rain God, this *cenote*, or natural well, is located at the end of a 300 meter-long avenue which goes south to the great plaza of El Castillo.

The water lies 22 meters below the rim of the well, and the well water itself varies in depth from 13 to 20 meters. The bottom consists of a muddy sediment of as much as 4 meters thick in places. The pool has an overall diameter of 60 meters. Algae and other

The Sacred Cenote and what remains
of the platform.

micro-organisms give the pool varying tones of green. The walls
are partly in their natural state, but on the south there is evidence
of human handiwork, as it must have been equipped with a series
of stepped platforms to accommodate the public who attended
the continuous ceremonies that were carried out in that place.

This cenote was set apart as sacred. Here were enacted the human sacrifices, where warriors, children and maidens were
thrown into the mysterious depths below from an irregular platform which almost jutted out from the rim. Next to the well is a
temazcal (steam bath), where the victims were purified before
being sacrificed.

During the period from 1882 to 1968, and using various systems
and techniques, several explorations of the depths of this pool
were made, and valuable objects and archaeological artifacts
have been recovered. These bear witness to the pilgrimages
of people from as far away as Panama, who came to leave their
offerings in the cenote. Among the objects retrieved are carvings
of serpent heads and tails; banner holders in the form of jaguars
and other feline animals; carved stones from the Ball Court; human skulls and hundreds of bones; wooden objects such as
benches, handles and a staff of authority; bells of gold, gold-
and-copper alloy, and copper; plaques and beads of jade; pyrite
disks and mirrors; rings and sandals of gilt copper; balls of copal
gum and rubber; vessels, pots and amphoras; some arrowheads,
and a number of beautifully engraved golden disks.

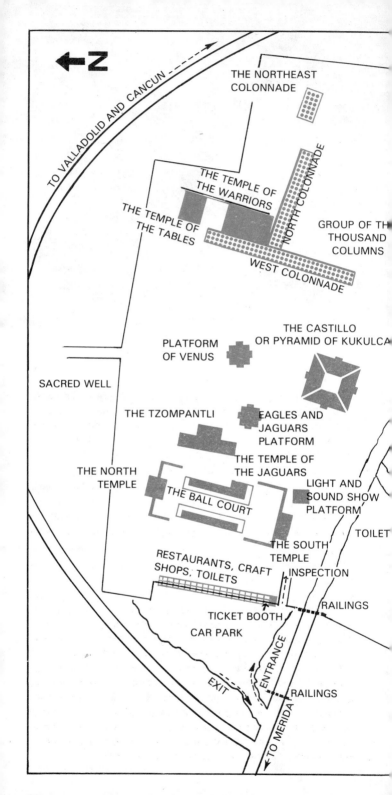

←N

TO VALLADOLID AND CANCUN

THE NORTHEAST
COLONNADE

THE TEMPLE OF
THE WARRIORS

THE TEMPLE OF
THE TABLES

NORTH COLONNADE

GROUP OF TH
THOUSAND
COLUMNS

WEST COLONNADE

THE CASTILLO
OR PYRAMID OF KUKULCA

PLATFORM
OF VENUS

SACRED WELL

THE TZOMPANTLI

EAGLES AND
JAGUARS
PLATFORM

THE TEMPLE OF
THE JAGUARS

THE NORTH
TEMPLE

THE BALL COURT

LIGHT AND
SOUND SHOW
PLATFORM

TOILET

THE SOUTH
TEMPLE

RESTAURANTS, CRAFT
SHOPS, TOILETS

INSPECTION

RAILINGS

TICKET BOOTH

CAR PARK

ENTRANCE

EXIT

RAILINGS

TO MERIDA

34

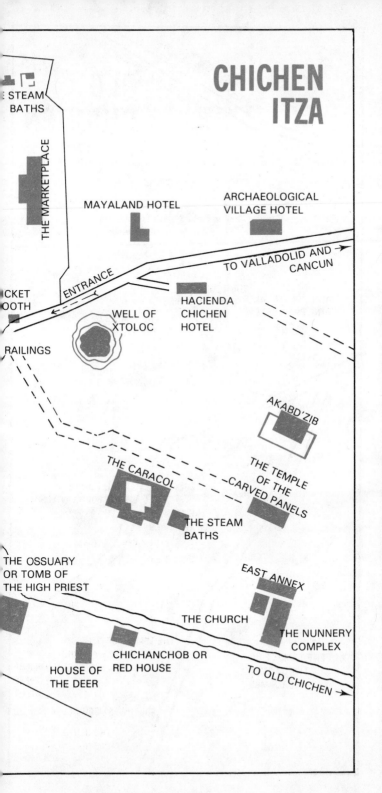

CHICHEN ITZA

STEAM BATHS

THE MARKETPLACE

MAYALAND HOTEL

ARCHAEOLOGICAL VILLAGE HOTEL

ENTRANCE

TO VALLADOLID AND CANCUN

TICKET BOOTH

WELL OF XTOLOC

HACIENDA CHICHEN HOTEL

RAILINGS

AKABD'ZIB

THE CARACOL

THE TEMPLE OF THE CARVED PANELS

THE STEAM BATHS

THE OSSUARY OR TOMB OF THE HIGH PRIEST

EAST ANNEX

THE CHURCH

THE NUNNERY COMPLEX

CHICHANCHOB OR RED HOUSE

HOUSE OF THE DEER

TO OLD CHICHEN

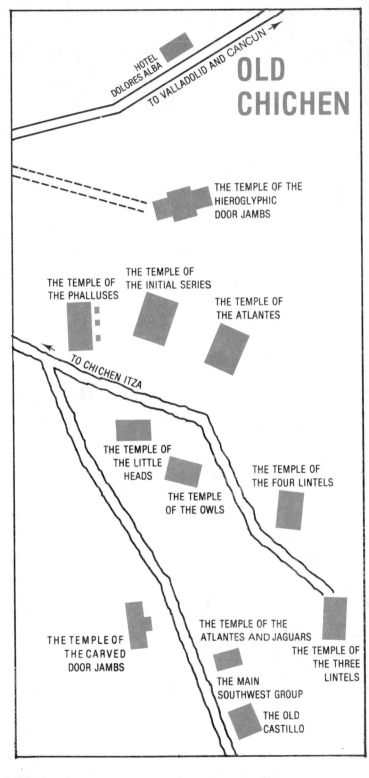

HOTEL DOLORES ALBA

TO VALLADOLID AND CANCUN →

OLD CHICHEN

THE TEMPLE OF THE HIEROGLYPHIC DOOR JAMBS

THE TEMPLE OF THE PHALLUSES

THE TEMPLE OF THE INITIAL SERIES

THE TEMPLE OF THE ATLANTES

TO CHICHEN ITZA

THE TEMPLE OF THE LITTLE HEADS

THE TEMPLE OF THE OWLS

THE TEMPLE OF THE FOUR LINTELS

THE TEMPLE OF THE CARVED DOOR JAMBS

THE TEMPLE OF THE ATLANTES AND JAGUARS

THE MAIN SOUTHWEST GROUP

THE OLD CASTILLO

THE TEMPLE OF THE THREE LINTELS

The road to Chichén Itzá.

Old Chichén

In the section known as Old Chichén, apart from the Cenote of Xtoloc, there is a grouping of numerous temples, some of which are in ruins. These include the Group of the Dates, the Temple of the Phalluses, the Temple of the Little Heads, the Temple of the Caryatids, the Temple of the Atlantes, the Temple of the Owls, the Temple of the Carved Door Jambs, the Temple of the Hieroglyphic Door Jambs, the Temple of the Four Lintels, the Temple of the Turtle, the Group of the Bird Cornice, and the Main Southwest Group.

Classic
Period
(600-900 A. D.)

Chichanchob
or Red House

The explanation of this name is the red-painted border on the face of the portico, although the structure is also known as Chichanchob ("little holes" in Maya), a name which refers to the openwork of the cresting.

On the facade of the Chichanchob one can observe the classicism of the Puuc style.

The temple stands on a raised foundation, rounded at the corners with a stairway on the west side. In the vestibule, where the vault begins, there is a row of carved hieroglyphs (a great part of them is worn away). A date, however, has been deciphered, which corresponds approximately to the year 870 A.D.

The interior contains two corridors, one forming a kind of vestibule and the other a kind of sanctuary consisting of three chambers, all with Classic Maya vaulting. The facade shows the sobriety of the Puuc style: unadorned friezes, two cornices with moldings, and stone lintels over doorways. This structure is characterized by its double cresting. The plastic motif of the older of the two is seen in the openwork frets between the entablatures; the second cresting, built somewhat later, repeats the motif of the frets, but with masks of the god Chac over the doorways.

Akab Dzib

The name of this structure, translated literally, means "obscure writing". The central edifice rests upon a low platform. It contains two rooms, and at the north and south ends are identical buildings with eight corridors roofed over with Maya vaults or false arches which give this interior space an air of seclusion and austerity. The structure as a whole includes three sections with eighteen chambers. The architectural style is sober, with plain friezes, doorways with unadorned stone lintels and jambs which give a pure, lineal aesthetic feeling. The wall of the facade has a cresting which accentuates its decorative elegance, and geometric fretwork of stone mosaic, which is characteristic of the Puuc style. The entrance in the south facade has a stone lintel on which is sculptured a priest sitting on a throne before a brazier, symbolizing fire worship. He is surrounded by a series of undeciphered hieroglyphics, thus the name "obscure writing" given the building. Some of the vaulted interiors are covered with a number of hand prints, painted red. These possibly symbolize Ke-

The House of the Deer.

bul, "celestial and creative hand", which is one of the terms of address for the god Itzamná. From the few signs on the lintel that have been deciphered, the experts have assigned it the date 869 A.D.

House of the Deer

The House of the Deer is situated a short distance from Chinchánchob, and shows very similar characteristics. It stands on a platorm with rounded corners and is ascended by a central stairway. According to tradition, it bears this name because there had once been a mural painting of a deer on one of the walls.

This little temple consists of a gallery divided into three chambers. The facade is completely without decoration, with a frieze between the moldings, and finished off at the front with undecorated cresting.

The Nunnery

This structure is the greatest monument of the Classic Period. It gets its name from the fact that its many rooms reminded the Spaniards of a convent, and from the information obtained by Bishop Landa about the existence of priestesses among the Maya, who lived there and participated in certain rites. The Nunnery consists of several superimposed architectural structures from various periods, in which the Chenes and Puuc styles have been identified.

First the foundation was built, measuring some 20 meters by 13 meters, with rounded corners, and with a height of 8 meters. This original foundation was later enlarged to measure 33 by 21 meters, 10 meters high, set on a flat base, with a smooth frieze between two moldings on the upper part. A stairway 17 meters wide flanked by smooth balustrades leads to the upper platform. Additions were subsequently added to the south, east, and west sides, increasing the surface dimensions to 50 by 27 meters, but keeping the same height. In the upper part the new annex ends in a frieze bordered by two moldings and adorned with masks of the god Chac, alternating with panels of latticework. Finally, still another construction was superimposed: a stairway not as wide

General view of the Nunnery complex.

as the previous one, with balustrades having perpendicular rings. This detail is unique in Mayan architecture. This stairway leads to a second floor, the center of which is interrrupted by a small construction. In a much more ruined state than the rest of the complex, the upper building consists of a single corridor with a door facing north.

The facade is decorated with a frieze of little columns between two cornices.

On the terrace and on each side of a second flight of stairs is a temple containing two long parallel galleries, each having six rooms, five on the north side and five on the south, with two separate rooms added on the ends, all of them with Maya vaulting.

The north facade is decorated with latticework, little columns and square figures. The south facade has fretwork rather than latticework, but has the same type of little columns and square figures, with carved rose-like figures added.

In the most recent platform there is a wide gap, attributed to the dynamite used by Le Plongeon in his exploration of the building, which exposed the original foundation. The gap is kept in that way so that the different construction periods can be appreciated.

Annex of the Nunnery

This is one of the most beautiful buildings of the Chenes style of Chichén Itzá. Added on to the last foundation of the complex, it consists of a rectangular ground plan made up of three parallel galleries, each containing two rooms, plus two additional chambers facing east and west, respectively.

The north and south facades are decorated with panels of latticework. The two front corners end in masks of the god Chac. In the frieze framed by moldings, the Chac masks are repeated on a smaller scale. Between the two upper moldings and running around the entire building there is a stone carving representing the undulating body of a serpent.

The facade of the east face of the building is very richly decorated, with a profusion of masks and figures shaped like hooked noses, all symbolizing Chac, god of rain. Because of their placement around the door, they give the impression that access is ef-

The beautiful facade of the Nunnery Annex.

fected through open fangs—possibly related to the idea of travel to the divine world.

In the upper part of the molding, doubled at an angle over the entranceway, there is a medallion framed by fretwork, in the center of which is depicted a seated personage with a splendid feather headdress.

The allegories of the rattlesnake tail that crown the moldings of the north and south facades lead one to suppose them to be more recent decorative additions.

Above the door there is a carved lintel, inscribed with hieroglyphics that the experts believe to date from the year 880 A.D.

The entire building is lined with a molding with cornice, and it is possible that at one time it was finished off with a frontal cresting, as seen in the drawing made on the spot by Frederick Catherwood in 1841. The overall composition of the building is very harmonious and esthetically pleasing.

The Church

This structure received its name because of its proximity to the Nunnery. It dates from the Puuc period (7th and 8th centuries, A.D.) It consists of a single vaulted room of rectangular ground plan, with an access door on the west. It is decorated profusely and symmetrically in stone mosaic. As a principal motif, the frieze on the facade displays three masks of Chac, the Rain God, at center and corners, with stylized hooked nose in bold relief. These are alternated with other masks, in pairs, which are identified with the four "bacabs", or "sustainers of the sky", here represented as the armadillo, the snail, the turtle and the crab, which differ from each other in accordance with the course each follows in the universe. In the lower part, the frieze is bordered by a molding of stepped frets, a motif that is repeated at the base of the cresting. In the upper part stretches a serpentine figure. Three masks of Chac project from the top of the cresting.

The sides of the building and the back wall of the facade are also decorated with masks, frets and a toothed border at the cor-

The large masks of the god Chac adorn the front and sides of the building of the Church.

47

nice, but they lack the elaborate decoration of the front of the building.

The Temple of the Three Lintels

The characteristics of this building make it a splendid example of the structures of the Maya Classic Period. It rests upon a base whose projecting moldings, lattices, frets and small masks enhance its rectangular shape. There are three chambers, each with a doorway topped with a sculptured lintel. One of these has been assigned the approximate date of 850 A.D., but this has not been duly verified. The lower part of the facade is unadorned, and the corners are rounded off with harmonious columns.

The stone carving between the two moldings, whose design simulates the undulating movement of a serpent, initiates the decoration of the upper part. The frontal lattice is decorated with bundles of four columns embedded in the wall, and masks of the Rain God Chac on the two corners complete the composition.

At the rear the only decoration consists of some latticed panels with small columns at the corners of the temple, which is finished off with a molding. This temple is located in Old Chichén, and has been totally reconstructed.

The Temple of the Four Lintels

This structure is located quite near the Temple of the Lintel. It is in extremely ruinous condition, but the stone lintels of the inner and outer doors still rise from the rubble. The lintels have carvings of calendrical glyphs, as yet undeciphered with exactitude. They surely must record some important event. Experts have assigned the date 889 A.D. to the construction of this building.

The harmonious structure of the Temple of the Three Lintels.

Calendrical glyphs carved on the Temple of the Four Lintels.

Transitional Period

(900-1000 A. D.)

The Caracol or Astronomical Observatory

The Maya were aware of the position of celestial bodies and observed their movements. Astronomy enabled them to devise a perfect calendar and to perform other scientific tasks. For this purpose they constructed observatories, the most distinctive of which is the Caracol structure at Chichén Itzá.

It consists of a rectangular platform measuring 67 meters from north to south and 52 meters from east to west. It is 6 meters

General view of El Caracol.

high, consists of one sloping-sided body with a cornice of rounded corners. Is has a stairway flanked by balustrades decorated with entwined serpents. On the original foundation was built a round structure 11 meters in diameter and 3.70 meters high, with molded cornices and masks of Chac, God of Rain. This round base sustains a third structure, also round in shape, which is 16 meters in diameter and 5 meters high, consisting of a single body of sloping blocks, projecting molding and a vertical wall finished off with another molding. In front of it is an attached terrace, 20 meters long and 6.5 meters wide, with a vertical wall finished with a molding similar to the above-mentioned one, which was covered by another terrace of slightly irregular shape, measuring 24 meters on its longest side, and surrounded by numerous stone incense-burners shaped like human heads. Some of these terraces are Maya constructions, and others show later modifications, especially those with sloping or inclined walls. On top of them ri-

SUMMER SOLSTICE EQUINOX

Lines of visión for watching the
sunset from the Observatory.

ses the cylindrical structure that constitutes the observation
chamber itself. This tower rises from the first or lower foundation, and shows that it originally consisted of a simple nucleus
that already had the spiral staircase or "caracol" that gives the
building its name. This staircase led to the observation chamber,
but subsequently, with the construction of the other foundations
with larger diameters, the nucleus was expanded with another
ring-shaped chamber, and finally, the terrace that now surrounds
the tower was built.

A spiral staircase leads to the observatory of this complex edifice. The small room above, with its sighting embrasures, enables
one to imagine how the Maya astronomers used to observe the
movements of the stars.

The Temple of the Phalluses

The fact that this building contains several rooms makes one
think that it might have been used for residential purposes. As
part of the "Group of the Dates," it definitely pertains to the Maya Classic Period. On the other hand, the sculptured phalluses
that are attached to the walls of the interior rooms, and which de-
rive from other Middle American cultural influences, are from a later period.

The Tower of the Observatory.

The Temple of the Phalluses.

General view of the Temple of the Warriors. To
the left can be seen the Temple of the Tables and
a large part of the Group of the Thousand Columns.

Maya - Toltec Period

(1000 - 1250 A. D.)

The Temple of the Warriors

This splendid edifice is situated in the rear area of the beautifully
carved pilasters of the West Colonnade. In large part it was constructed on top of a more ancient temple known as the Chac-
Mool. The foundation measures 40 meters per side and is 12 meters high. It has several set-back levels with sloping sides and a
cornice that is profusely carved with warriors, jaguars and eagles
devouring human hearts—typical Toltec elements. The Temple,

Sectional view of the structure of the Temple
of the Warriors.

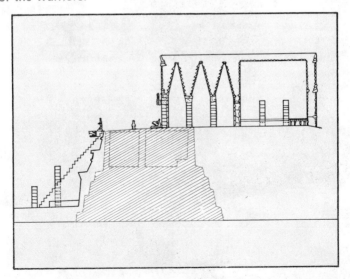

High reliefs on the Temple of the Warriors.

which measures 21 meters per side and contains two chambers, is reached by a stairway flanked by balustrades with carved plumed serpents. Over their heads, which finish off the upper part of the stairway, are the warrior carvings that served as banner holders.

Opposite the portico of the Temple there is a wide platform, on which there is a sculpture of a Chac-Mool between two pilasters in the shape of magnificently decorated plumed serpents, whose heads reach the floor level. The serpent tails support the lintels of the entranceway.

Access to the first chamber of the Temple is through the three openings between the two pilasters. The entranceways have carved door jambs. The pilasters, located inside, carved with the image of Kukulcán, warriors and other important personages, held up the beams that supported the vaulted roof. In addition to the pilasters that held up the roof, in the second chamber there is an altar supported by sculptures of "atlantes" and attached to the rear wall.

On the exterior walls of the Temple, Maya and Toltec religious motifs are mingled.

Altar supported by Atlantes. Temple of the Warriors.

Chac-Mool and pilaster in the portico of the Temple of the Warriors. On the lateral part are motifs that refer to the god Chac and to Kukulcán-Quetzalcóatl.

Base of the balustrade of the stairway.
Temple of the Warriors.

Over the cornice that ends the slope of the lower part are the typical Puuc-style masks of the Rain God, Chac, and a high relief with the human face of Kukulcán-Quetzalcóatl emerging from the jaws of a serpent. The whole composition reposes on a low relief representing the feathers and claws of a bird.

As one comes out of the temple building and walks along the upper platform, one comes upon a stairway that leads to two vaulted chambers that formed part of the oldest structure. This is the substructure of the Warriors, or Temple of Chac-Mool, so called because a sculpture of that type was found there.

Originally the walls of this chamber were decorated with mural paintings. Although they are in very poor condition on account of the climate and environment, one can still make out some scenes with warriors and priests lined up with offerings, and other personages seated on thrones covered with jaguar skins and other elements that are hard to identify.

Carved pilasters with warriors and personages.
Temple of the Warriors.

The North Colonnade.

Group of the
Thousand Columns

Located in the Maya-Toltec section of Chichén, this group gets its name from the profusion of columns and pillars that surround a large rectangular plaza measuring 150 meters on each side, which has still not been completely explored.

Outstanding among the buildings that make up this enormous complex are the Temple of the Warriors, the Marketplace, the north and west Colonnades and the Steam Bath. In the subsoil of the plaza there are a large number of unexplored ruined structures.

A large part of the columns and capitals of this architectural complex served to support the beams that held up the stone vaulting. Because of its magnificence, it must have stood out even during Chichén Itzá's period of greatest splendor.

The columns and pillars that comprise the Group of the Thousand Columns, many of which are beautifully carved, are located in different parts of the area, as indicated by the names North, Northeast, East, Southeast, West and Northwest Colonnades.

The Northeast Colonnade.

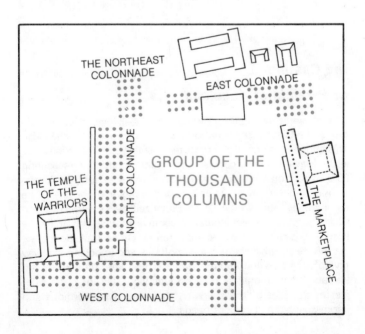

The Castillo
or Pyramid of Kukulcán

Because of its location, but above all, because of its magnificence, the Castillo stands out over all the buildings of Chichén Itzá. This structure is one of the most representative of Toltec influence in the Maya region. It consists of a square foundation measuring 55.5 meters on each side, which supports nine set-back levels, symbolizing the way to the underworld or region of the dead. The pyramid, 24 meters high, is characterized by sloping sides and slightly projecting rectangular decorative motifs, similar to the scapulary panels of Zapotec architecture. On each of the four sides of the pyramid there is a sumptuous and imposing stairway giving access to the Temple above. These are bordered by balustrades that emphasize their esthetic vigor. On the north side, just at the foot of the stairway, there are two enormous and impressive plumed-serpent heads.

The Castillo in the most imposing building at Chichén Itzá.

STRUCTURES OF "EL CASTILLO"

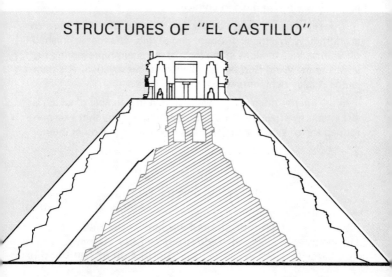

The temple proper is a vestibule with three entrance openings, separated by two columns that represent serpents with open jaws their heads form the base of the columns, their bodies the shaft, and their tails curve in such a way as to serve as capitals supporting the wooden lintel of the doorways. The interior chamber is vaulted and has two pilasters decorated in low relief, which support the beams or rafters of the roof. At the back of the sanctuary is a narrow gallery with three doors leading to the west, south and east stairways. The motif of this temple is an inclined or sloping wall, which also has a flat, vertical wall surmounted by a frieze between two molded cornices.

Three inset panels appear on the central border. The main entrance is adorned with a mask of Chac, god of rain. The roof is finished off with various merlons in the form of cut snails representing the jewels of the Wind God, an appellation of Quetzalcóatl. The door jambs display richly attired warriors and priests.

In the interior there is a smaller pyramid, the temple of which is still intact, even with vestiges of the last ceremony that was performed there. When archaeologists discovered this other interior

The Chac-Mool and the Red Jaguar in the inner Temple of the Castillo.

Head of plumed serpent at the base of one of the balustrades of the stairways on the north side of The Castillo.

world, they found there a throne, in the form of a red-painted jaguar, whose spots are encrusted jade disks, and a Chac-Mool placed at the former entrance, at the very top of the hidden stairway. Under the outer masonry shell of the exterior pyramid were found carvings decorating the facade. This inner structure was one of the first built by the Toltecs in Yucatan, and is evidence of the religious custom of building a larger temple, or pyramid, superimposed over a smaller one, at the end of each 52-year cycle.

The Mexican expert Luis E. Arochi, who began his research at Chichén Itzá in 1972, deduced that the larger pyramid had been built for astronomical purposes — a deduction corroborated by the spring and autumn equinoxes (March 20 and September 21).

At about 3 p.m. on those dates, sunlight is projected on the wall of the balustrade on the northwest side, immediately forming a wavy motion or undulation. As the sun drops lower in the sky, seven isosceles triangles of light and shadow are formed, from top to bottom, which form the body of a huge serpent more than 34 meters long. The triangles join at the head of the serpent situated at the foot of the balustrade.

This singular effect of light and shadow — which these days attracts thousands of visitors to Chichen to observe it — has been identified by Arochi as ''the symbolic descent of Kukulcán'', plumed serpent, perhaps signifying the start of the agricultural cycle in March.

The same expert has proved that when the full moon is in a similar position to that of the sun during the equinoxes, at about three o'clock, moonlight forms seven triangles on the pyramid, similar to those formed by sunlight at the times of the equinox.

The Temple of the Tables

At the north side of the Temple of the Warriors stands the Temple of the Tables. It is a pyramid in a very ruined state, and is nine meters high. The pilasters, with beautifully carved personages in the upper portion, frame the entrances to the Temple. Altars composed of stone slabs upheld by sculptured ''atlantes'' (only one of which is still in upright position) complete the remaining elements of the structure.

Altar and pilasters of the Temple of the Tables.

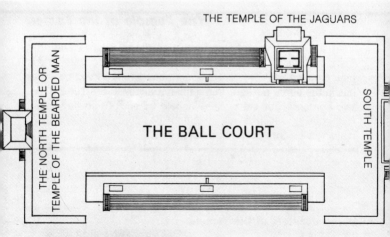

The Ball Court

Ball games were common among many pre-Columbian peoples. The sacred book of the Maya, the *Popol Vuh*, mentions them. They had both a sporting and a religious purpose.

The competing teams played with balls made of hard rubber. Players used their elbows, knees and hips to hit the ball. Victory consisted of manoeuvering the ball through the stone rings that were attached to the walls of the court. Religious ceremonies and rites also took place on occasions when games were played.

The main Ball Court is located beyond the western part of the great esplanade that surrounds the Castillo.(There are at least six

The Ball Court seen from the South Temple.

other ball courts at Chichén Itzá). The main Court consists of a rectangular structure 168 meters long and 70 meters wide. It is bordered by two long terraces, except on the ends, where it is wider and takes the characteristic shape of ball courts in other Middle American cultures: a double "I" bordered by walls.

Sculptured relief on one of the two lateral walls of the Ball Court. The players of the two teams were separated by the skull representing death, and out of whose mouth came the symbol of the word. The player on the left is holding a stone knife in one hand, and in the other the head of the captain of the opposing team, whom he has just decapitated. Blood gushes from the neck of the sacrificial victim symbolized by a bunch of serpents.

Detail of one of the symbols of death.

**Rear view of the Temple
of the Jaguars with its annex.**

Stairways with balustrade borders led to the upper levels, where there were small structures, possibly used as tribunes or speaking platforms for important people like judges.

In the middle of each of the two 8-meter-high side walls of the
court are attached the stone rings for the game, carved with
coiled plumed serpents representing Kukulcán-Quetzalcóatl.

All along the lower part of the bordering terraces of the court
are slanting benches decorated with carved panels in low relief,
showing the players in full regalia, making their way in a proces-
sion toward a central motif: the symbol of death. The first player
in the line on the right is kneeling and has just been decapitated.
Out of his body blood is gushing in the form of serpents and
garlands of leaves and flowers. The first player in the line on the
left faces the decapitated player (the captain of the opposing
team). In one hand he is holding his victim's head, and in the
other the obsidian knife used in the sacrifice. Above these reliefs

The entrance to the Temple of the Jaguars.

runs a molding of a serpent, whose head extends to the ends of the bench. The scene shows the importance that these ball games had, for the victor won the privilege of offering his life to the gods. At the same time, it suggests the fertility of the land.

The Temple of the Jaguars

An inclined column base was erected in a break in the long western platform of the ball court and a narrow stairway located on the south side led up to the top of the platform.

A further section was built at this level, giving access to the temple by means of a staircase of which the struts were engraved in relief with designs alluding to Kukulcán.

Access to the temple is assured by three entrances formed by two splendid columns in the shape of snakes, their heads forming

the column bases. Their tails support the lintels of the entrances and both the lintels and door jambs are decorated with warrior motifs.

The body of the temple is made up of a vestibule and a room containing an altar, serving as a sanctuary. One enters through a door with a wooden lintel; the jambs are decorated with warrior figures. Within, traces of mural paintings are visible. The most impressive, with a wealth of detail, is the representation of one of the major battles waged by the Itzá tribe.

**Mural painting representing a battle,
Temple of the Jaguars.
National Museum of Anthropology copy.**

The frieze in the lower part of the temple is adorned with intertwined serpents and the central band features the rampant jaguars which gave the building its name. The jaguars are seen walking in opposite directions towards three interposed shields which are the symbol of war. In the upper section we see the undulating forms of two plumed serpents with their tails entwined. Further decorative elements were added in the spaces left open by the undulations of the serpents' bodies.

A carved stone seat representing a jaguar is found in the middle of the entranceway of the annex.

Annex to the Temple of the Jaguars

This small structure is on the same level as the great square and is adjacent to the back side of the foundation of the Temple of the Jaguars. It is a one-room structure with three entrances, which in turn consist of two pilasters and a vaulted roof. In the entranceway between the two pilasters there is a carved stone seat in the form of a jaguar.

The front of the building is composed of a frieze between two cornices. The walls are ornately decorated with figures of warriors and with panels on which Kukulcán appears as bird-serpent-man. The entrance pilasters were carved with the same decorations, although in this case Kukulcán assumed a different form on the entrance door jambs. The interior walls and the vault are carved with many warriors and other important figures, all elaborately attired, which blended into the overall scene by means of whorls, plants and other decorative elements.

The North Temple or the Temple of the Bearded Man

This structure, which was built after the Ball Court, is elaborately decorated in low relief. It has a 14-meter by 8-meter platform attached to the north wall which borders the Ball Court. The

The North Temple, so called because of its location within the Ball Court, is also known as the Temple of the Bearded Man, because of a low relief in the center of the back wall.

platform supports the foundation of three levels with sloping walls. The stairway that leads up from the center faces south and is bordered by balustrades decorated with "trees of life". The trees are profusely adorned with flowers, butterflies and rare birds that receive their sustenance from the Monster of the Earth. On a panel above these trees appears an effigy of the Man-Bird-Serpent (Kukulcán).

The Temple is ten meters long by six meters wide and has only one room with a vaulted roof. It is profusely decorated with various religious scenes and scenes from everyday life. The columns are decorated with a series of warriors in low relief. Also in low relief at one end of the building is the composition that gives its name to the Temple—the head of a bearded man. Among the many ornamental figures is Kukulcán, an imposing presence on his jaguar throne, surrounded by a plumed serpent. On either side of the deity are seven warriors holding dart throwers (atlatl). In another row Kukulcán appears again, this time elaborately dressed. The *chalchihuites*, or precious stones, that adorn his robe symbolize his dignity and high rank. He is accompanied by thirteen seated figures, seven on his left and six on his right. Beneath Kukulcán is a row of eagle-men, two of whom are standing above a temple, in the interior of which are two seated figures. Kukulcán lies below, protected by a two-headed serpent and by the *Bacabs* that held up the heavens at the four cardinal points.

The South Temple

The South Temple was attached to the south end of the Ball Court, which had been built previously.

This one-room structure, which measures 25 meters by 8 meters, has no decoration on the facade, but has a cornice between the moldings and the frieze. The six pilasters that make up the seven entrance openings are decorated with figures of warriors; on the part above them are hieroglyphics in which appear the names of the warriors. On the lower panels the Man-Bird-Serpent is represented as emerging from the jaws of a plumed serpent—an image that represents the governing authority who assumes the form of the deity Kukulcán.

A surprising acoustic phenomenon is the fact that when one speaks in this Temple, one's voice can be heard in the Temple of the Bearded Man, which is located at the opposite end of the Ball Court, and from the walls of which the sound waves bounce back.

To the south of the Ball Court is the Temple that bears this name.

The South Temple has handsomely carved pilasters with personages and warriors in the upper part, and representations of Kukulcán in the lower part.

The Tzompantli

This monument is the one that most clearly alludes to the human sacrifices carried out according to the warrior-religious mystique of the cultures of the Central Highlands of Mexico. The "Tzompantli," which literally means "wall of skulls," is a rectangular platform 60 meters long and 12 meters wide. A stairway leads up to a structure that projects from the east facade. The building is adorned with symbols of death, and on a low slope are a cornice, a panel and another cornice, decorated with relief carvings of skulls impaled on stakes, as was the custom followed with the heads of sacrificial victims. The cornices are capped with serpent coils. The ornamentation is completed by eagles devouring hearts, warriors and plumed serpents, which leads to the supposition that the skulls of sacrificial victims were displayed on the Tzompantli.

Excavations carried out on this platform have brought to light offerings, human skulls, and two Chac-Mools.

The theme human sacrifice in evident in the decoration of The Tzompantli.

Detail of the reliefs on one of the walls.

The Platform of Venus

This structure consists of a square platform with access steps up each side, flanked by low balustrades whose upper portions terminate in immense heads of plumed serpents with bodies extending the length of the panels. The sloped side is composed of panels on different levels. The projecting panels have carved allegorical figures of the planet Venus in the form of a bundle of years, associated with a Venusian flower with cross pieces on its petals, indicating the month "pop," and a braided stele symbolizing power. From the recessed slabs or panels Venus rises from the opened jaws of a ser-

In the reliefs on the Platform of Venus the allegories of the planet Venus and to Kukulcán are outstanding.

pent representing Kukulcán. This image signifies that Venus was one of the names given to the plumed serpent.

Emblems of the serpent extend the full length of the cornice panels, and among the undulating coils are carvings of fish.

The Temple of Venus is also known as the "Tomb of the Chac-Mool," since Le Plongeon found here a sculpture of that type, which is now exhibited in the National Museum of Anthropology and History in Mexico City.

Bishop Landa mentions that this platform was possibly used for holding different kinds of spectacles or performances, such as dances.

The Temple of the Eagles and Jaguars

This Temple has the same architectural characteristics as the Temple of Venus: a rectangular ground plan and flights of steps on both sides, finished off at the top with great plumed serpent heads.

On the outwardly projecting panels the relief carving represents eagles devouring human hearts, whereas the inward receding panels show jaguars in the same position. The jaguars have beautifully decorated spots.

These images are concerned with the sun's journey across the heavenly vault by day, and with Tlalchitonatiuh, "sun of earth," in its descent into the underworld during the night. The eagles and jaguars allude to the warriors who captured victims for the sun god.

On the upper cornice are carved figures of recumbent warriors, which possibly symbolize Kukulcán.

An eagle eating human hearts.
Detail of the decoration of the Temple of
the Eagles and Jaguars.

The slender columns of
the Marketplace.

The Marketplace

Although called the marketplace, there is no concrete evidence proving that this builidng was used for such a purpose.

Located south of the group of the Thousand Columns, this structure stands on a low platform, with one central and two lateral stairways leading up to it.

The principal chamber is composed of a gallery with high walls at the rear, and columns and pillars at the sides and front. A stone bench runs the length of the back wall. Near the entrance there is an altar with a base decorated with human figures and plumed serpents along the cornice. Pilasters with carvings of personages of Chichén Itzá (warriors and priests) decorate the entrance way.

At the back of the gallery, tall slender columns formed a rectangular courtyard 17 meters square. The consistency of the columns leads one to suppose that they supported a light roof, probably constructed of rafters and palm leaves.

A row of clam shells and a cut conch shell (a valuable trinket symbolic of Ehécatl, the Wind God) complete the decoration of the facade.

The steam bath located near the Marketplace.

The Steam Baths

Near the Marketplace there is a steam bath, or sweathouse. The portico, with four columns and benches affixed to the walls, served as a waiting room. The entrance to the steam room as such was through a small, narrow, low-roofed door.

Two stone benches along the side served as places for bathers to rest. In the kiln or oven at the rear, stones were heated red hot, after which they were placed in an intermediate passageway where cold water was poured over them to produce dense steam.

Drainage was effected through a pipe, and smoke and steam were eliminated through apertures in the upper part of the walls.

This type of bath was used not only for ordinary bathing but also for ritualistic and medicinal purposes.

There are two other steam baths at Chichén Itzá. One of them is located in the south part of the Caracol or Observatory. This structure, which is in a very ruined state, is made up of a portico with columns, and a steam room with benches. The other steam bath is located on the south rim of the Sacred Cenote, but only remnants of the structure remain.

It is conjectured that in this steam bath were purified the victims who were periodically thrown into the waters of the cenote as propitiatory offerings to the gods.

The Temple of the Carved Panels

This Temple is located on the east side of the great plaza, flanked by the Caracol and the Nunnery. Its construction embraces two different periods. On a foundation was first built the Temple, of some 10 meters long by 6 meters wide, consisting of a portico with three entranceways, with two columns in the form of serpents and an interior chamber with a bench. Another part was added on to the original construction at a later time. It consisted of an interior double line of columns and a bench running along the three walls. Access to it is through a portico with four columns.

The first stairway was torn down to build another one leading over the roof to the Temple. On the exterior lateral walls of the second construction are to be seen the carved panels which gave the Temple its name. The three rows of low reliefs of these panels are carved with varied motifs: a hut with three persons, warriors, gods, birds, serpents, jaguars, monkeys and trees.

The building as a whole is very similar to the Temple of the Warriors

The Ossuary

Also known as the Tomb of the High Priest, the Ossuary stands on a pyramid 10 meters high. On each side there are stairways with balustrades that are decorated with entwined serpents, ending in the upper parts in the heads of the same serpents. The entire complex has fallen into ruin.

It is composed of a central sanctuary surrounded by a gallery forming the portico. The pillars have carvings with human figures and plumed serpents. In the middle part of the first two pillars is an opening in the floor leading down to a well where seven successive tombs were found, and where had been deposited various offerings of jade, rock crystal, shells and copper bells. The walls were covered with projecting stones which served as steps,

General view of the Temple of the Carved Panels.

Detail of the Carved Panels with different motifs.

making it possible to climb down to ground level. From there one can go down through a narrow opening or crevice to a natural cave that is lower than the base of the pyramid, and which is related to the threshold of the World of the Dead and of Paradise. It is clear that during the Toltec period this funerary monument was used to bury people of high rank.

The Temple of the Initial Series

This Temple is in the so-called "Group of the Dates", which consists of several temples. It is considered to be of great importance because it has the only hieroglyphic inscription with a complete date in Old Chichén: "10.2.9.1.9., 9 Muluc 7 Zac," and another date, in abbreviated form: "10.210.0.0., 2 Ahau 13 Chen" —both dates correspond to the year 879 A.D.

This inscription, which belongs to the Maya Classic Period, is carved on a lintel that had later been placed over two huge "atlante" -style columns, in eminently Toltec style, which completed the foundation.

Maya date inscriptions usually begin with what is called the long count, or initial series. This series indicated how many *baktunes, katunes, tunes, uinales* and *kines* had gone by since the reference time.

In the Maya calendar the unit of time was the day (*kin*); 20 kins made up an *uinal* and 18 uinals a *tun*—that is, an incomplete year of 360 days; 20 *tuns* made up a *katun*, and 20 *katuns* made up a *baktun*—altogether a cycle of almost 400 years.

From *La civilización de los antiguos mayas* (The Civilization of the Ancient Maya), by Alberto Ruz L., Mexico City, INAH, 1953.)

The Temple of the Carved Door Jambs

This is a small building in an advanced state of deterioration. It has a portico and a sanctuary in which the most noteworthy decorations are the carved human figures on the door jambs of the entranceway.

On the upper part of the Ossuary the pilasters surround the entranceway to the well that contained the tombs of personages or priests.

The lintel with calendrical glyph carvings that give their name to the Temple of the Initial Series.

The Temple of the Atlantes

The two large "atlantes" that flank the entrance to this small building constitute its most notable decorative element. The position of their arms and hands would seem to indicate that they served to support the base of the roof. Their attire (nose pendants, bracelets, belts and breast plates) identifies them as warriors.

The Temple of the Little Heads

This Temple is a small structure that is in a deteriorated condition. It was covered by a vaulted roof held up by "atlante"-style columns. The name of the Temple derives from the little heads carved in stone that decorated the interior.

The Temple of the Owls

This temple is completely destroyed, and all that remains are some pilasters on which can be seen beautiful reliefs representing owls.

The sculptures in the Temple of the Atlantes are of Toltec origin.

High relief in the Temple of the Owls.

The Main Southwest Group

These buildings are located at the end of a long "sacbe" (road), and are practically in ruins. The complex includes several buildings constructed during the Maya-Toltec period. Among the more important structures of this group are the Castillo of Old Chichén, which, though less spectacular than the main Castillo, was built on top of a high pyramid, and the Temple of the Jaguars, where the influence of the ancient jaguar god cult inherited from the Olmecs is fused with the influence of the Toltecs as manifested in "atlante"-style columns, which problably represent tiger-men.

The Temple of the Hieroglyphic Door Jambs

It is common in Mayan architecture for door jambs to have low relief or hieroglyphic carving on them, such as that found on this building. The door jambs are the vertical pieces that hold up the arch of the door. This structure is in the form of a courtyard surrounded by galleries quite similar to, though smaller than the Marketplace. Situated in Old Chichén, this Temple is in an advanced state of deterioration and is covered with undergrowth.

Group of the Bird Cornice

Locating the exact position of this structure is difficult, since only fragments remain, hidden in the underbrush. The name comes from the decoration of disks and birds carved on a colonnade.

The Temple of the Turtle

Several stones from the facade of this building were found in the rubble. Some were in the form of vases and another in the form of a turtle, and it was from the latter that the building got its name. The frieze is decorated with a row of balusters joined together. It also has two porticos, one facing north and the other facing south. It consists of one corridor divided into three chambers. It is difficult to determine its exact location.

GLOSSARY

Architrave.
> The lowermost part of an entablature, resting directly on top of the capital of a column.

Bacabs.
> Mayan word used to describe human figures with certain features who symbolically held up the sky at its four cardinal points.

Balustrade.
> Term used to describe the row of stones bordering the stairways of various pre-Hispanic constructions.

Basamento.
> The part formed by the base and pedestal of a column.

Beam or rafter.
> A long, thick wooden beam.

Capital.
> The top part or head of a column or pillar, having different kinds of decorative figures, according to the architectural style to which it belongs.

Cenote.
> Natural water source from an underground course open to the surface in the form of a well or hollow, formed in the limestone floor of the Yucatan Peninsula.

Ceramics.
> The art of making and other objects out of clay; all kinds of pottery or porcelain; all such objects in general.

Chac.
> The Maya god of rain.

Chac Mool.
> A semi-recumbent sculptured figure with bent knees and inclined head, which some archaeologists define as the representation of the divine messenger between man and the gods.

Chultun.
> Mayan word used for describing the cistern in which rain water was kept.

Codex.

Ancient manuscript of historical or literary importance. Strictly speaking, codices are only those manuscripts that predate the invention of the printing press.

Column.

A supporting pillar consisting of a base, a cylindrical shaft, and a capital, whose purpose is to support roofs or other parts of a structure, or as decoration on buildings.

Colonnade.

A group of columns.

Cornice.

A horizontal molded projection that crowns or completes a building or wall. The uppermost part of an entablature. The molding at the top of the walls of a room, between the walls and ceiling.

Cresting.

Ornamental fretwork on the top of buildings, particularly the latticework decoration on pre-Hispanic constructions.

Dzono.

Maya word meaning *cenote*.

Entablature.

Group of moldings that crown an architectural structure.

Façade.

The exterior of a building.

Face or surface (of a wall).

Either of the two faces of a wall.

Fretwork or fret.

An ornamental design contained within a band or border, consisting of repeated decorative figures.

Frieze.

A horizontal part of an entablature between the architrave and cornice. Any decorative horizontal band, as along the upper part of a wall in a room.

Glyph.

A decorative grooved figure, engraved or incised in stone.

Jade.
> A very hard and durable mineral, usually light green in color, made, up of magnesium silicate and lime; many Stone Age tools were made of this material.

Jaguar.
> A large feline animal, a kind of American leopard having a black-spotted pelt.

Jamb.
> The two vertical pieces that support the lintel or arch of doors or windows.

Large mask.
> A fantastic ornament used as a decorative element in certain architectural works.

Latticework or lattice.
> An open framework or screen placed over windows or other openings in such a way that persons inside can see without being seen. Used as a decorative element in architecture.

Lintel.
> Upper part of doors, windows and other openings, resting on the jambs.

Low relief.
> Sculptural relief that projects very little from the background.

Merlon.
> Battlements built on the top of European fortresses or ramparts. Also applied to the decorative elements on the top of pre-Hispanic constructions.

Masonry.
> Stonework or brickwork made with mortar and irregular stones or blocks.

Molding.
> An embellishment in strip form used to decorate buildings or surfaces in architecture or carpentry.

Opening (as for a door).
> Part of a wall where there is no support for the roof, such as the openings for windows and doors and between columns.

Panel.

A flat, usually rectangular piece forming a part of a surface in which it is set, and being raised, recessed, or framed.

Pilaster.

Square column or buttress.

Portico.

A porch, vestibule or walkway with a roof supported by columns, often leading to the entrance of temples and other sumptuous edifices; a gallery with arcades or columns along a facade or patio.

Puuc.

Mayan word meaning "mountain range". Name given to a style of architecture.

Quetzal.

A beautifuly coloured bird which lives in the jungles of southern Mexico and Central America.

Quetzalcoatl.

Plumed serpent, bird serpent, quetzal-serpent. Originally a deity of Teotihuacan civilisation, later venerated throughout Meso-america. The god creator of the Fifth Sun, the wind (Ehecatl) and the new race of man. Preaching a religion of love, he taught peoples agriculture, metalwork and the use of the calendar; he established and set dates for ceremonies and sacrifices; he proscribed human sacrifices. He furnished man with the means for studying the movement of heavenly bodies.

Rosette.

A circular adornment with various carved motifs.

Sacbé.

Maya word meaning "white road".

Sanctuary or shrine.

A sacred place or temple where the image or relic of god is worshipped.

Shaft.

The main body of a column, between the base and the capital.

Sloping or inclined wall (talud).

The sloping surface of a wall or land.

Solid wall.

Wall without apertures or openings; in architecture, the part of a wall between two openings.

Stele or stela.

An upright stone or slab with an inscribed or sculptured surface, used as a monument or as a commemorative tablet.

Stucco.

A mixture of cement, sand and lime, applied wet and forming a durable finish for exterior walls.

Sub.

The term usually means "beneath";

Tablero.

A projecting decorative surface on some parts of a building; the flat upper part of the capital.

Printed in:
Edicupes, S.A.
Av. San Lorenzo 251
Col. San Nicolás Tolentino
09850 México, D.F.
1000 copies
Mexico City, August, 1991